CONTENTS

Prayer for the fruit of the womb

Prayer against spiritual attack.

INTRODUCTION

"Confess your faults one to another and pray and pray one for another that ye may be healed the effectual fervent prayer of a righteous man availed much (James 5:16) "For the eyes of the lord are over the righteous and, his ears are open unto their prayers, but the face of the lord is against them that do evil" (1 Peter3:16)

The two biblical verses above simply explain that prayer is important in the life of all Christians. they also tell us that for our prayers to receive quick respond, we must be righteous.

The first verse places conditions on the prayers that God answers the first condition is confession and the second is righteous. we must confess our sins.

The second verse tells us that God is always ready to listen to us whenever we come to him in prayer. The verse advises us to avoid and run away from evil, and to come to God, and not to man in our moments or tribulation. You can accomplish more in an hour with god than one lifetime without him, prayer is spiritual or physical. Doing so, we will have all our problems sowed when any situation confronts us.

It is important for us to be on our knees all the time in this sinful world, the world in which Satan and his agent are in control. There is no way we can defeat Satan and its agents, in their domain without empowering yourselves with the weapon of prayer, we must therefore, pray hard to be victorious always. Therefore, pray without season.

MORNING PRAYER

PRAYER POINTS

1. Good morning, God the father, God the soil and God the Holy Spirit.

2. 1 thank you Lord, for the grace of sleeping peacefully last night and waking me hale and hearty this morning (Psalm 4:8)

3. Father accept my thanksgiving offering of waking up this orningpcacefu11Y in Jesus name (Lev. 22:29)

4. Angels of God protect and guide me in all my ways today (Psalm55: 16--17)

5. The Holy Spirit of God direct my ways,
   to where I will receive mercy, favour and
   blessing today in Jesus Name

6. 1 claim divine encounter in my place of
   work, office and business today in Jesus
   name.

7. 1 claim my divine package of goodness,
   love and mercy, in Jesus name
   (Rom.5:15, Gen 6:8)

8. Oh God of providers provide me my daily
   bread today and always and also to those
   Who are in need of same
   (Gen 22:8)

9. Oh God, let your mercy speak for mc in
   my dealings with any man/woman today
   in Jesus name (Number
   14:18)

10. Any man/Woman that may want to deny
    mc my right today shall fail, in Jesus
    name.

11. Any evil arrow of the enemy towards me shall return back to the sender, in Jesus name (Ps 141:10)

12. The blood of Jesus cover me and protect me from every physical or spiritual attack in Jesus name (Eph. 2: 13)

13. Anything I lay my hands on today shall be prosperous, today shall be like no other day to me in terms of successes, blessings promotions to next level and favour that I am going to receive, in Jesus name (Psalm 128:2, EccI.3:13)

14. Any evil holes that the enemy might have dug for me today, they shall be the one to fall in it in Jesus name.

15. Father, I thank you for your promise and grace of a blessed day (Num. 23:20)

16. I claim divine presence in my business, office and workshop today in Jesus name

17. Every evil arrow the enemy may direct at me today shall return to the sender in Jesus name (PS. 141:10)

18. I shall not lose any good thing today. I shall rather find favour in present of men

19. I shall go out and come back safely today in the mighty name of Jesus (Deut 2 8:6)

20. 1 reject any encounter with law enforcement agency that may restrict my freedom and cause me unnecessary financial spending today in Jesus name.

21. I claim divine blessings from the North, south, east and west today in Jesus name. (Ps *5:12)*

22. Father contend with those who will contend with me today (Isaiah 49:25)

EVENING PRAYER

(PRAYER POI NTS)

1. Thank you Lord, for my going out and coming in safely today (Ps. 12 1:8)

2. Father, I thank you, for not allowing any evil to happen to me through out today, and I know that no evil shall harm me tonight as well, in Jesus name (Ps 121:6)

3. Any evil eye that has been monitoring my movement since the sun broke today and is still monitoring me now, go blind in Jesus name.

4. All evil gathering against me this evening, I scatter you by fire, in Jesus name (Psalm 119:115)

5. All those who use the cover of the night to engage on their evil plans, die now, in Jesus name(Prov. 3:24)

6. Oh lord, help me to regain all the energy I have lost during the day as I rest my body to sleep tonight, in Jesus' name

7. 1 renounce and reject every covenant that brought reproach into my life in Jesus' name (Joshua 5:9)
8. I cancel all the evil plans to harm me in my dreams, in Jesus name.
9. I resist bad dreams, sweet dreams shall be my portion as I sleep tonight in Jesus name (Joel 2:28)
10. Every evil hands that pointed at me during the day, wither as the sun sets this evening, in Jesus name.

PSALM 91

He who dwells in the secret place of the most high shall abide under the shadow of the Almighty. I will say of the LORD, "He is my refuge and my fortress, my God, in Him I will trust".
Surely he shall deliver you from the snare of the fowler and from the perilous pestilence. He shall cover you with His

feathers, and under his wings you shall take refuge; His truth shall be your shield and bucker.

You shall not be afraid of the terror by night, nor of the arrow that flies by day, nor of the pestilence that walks in darkness, nor of the destruction that lays waste at noonday.

A thousand may fall at your side, and ten thousand at your right hand; but it shall not come near you only with your eyes shall you look, and see the reward of the wicked.

Because you have made the LORD, who is my refuge, even the most High, your dwelling place, no evil shall befall you, nor shall any plague come near your dwelling; for He shall give His angels charge over you, to keep you in all your ways.

In their hands they shall bear you up, lest you dash your foot against a stone. You shall tread upon the lion and the serpent you shall trample under foot. Me, therefore I will deliver him; I will set him on high, because he has known my name. He shall call upon me and I will answer him; I will be with him I trouble; I will deliver him and honor him. With long life I will satisfy him and show him my salvation.

PRAYER AGAINST ILLNESS

Bible Reading: Psalm 86, 3, 70, John 11:4, Exodus *25:25,* Proverb 18:14-15,Acts 10:38

Sing this song before saying this prayer

I am the God that healeth thee

I am the Lord your Healer

I sent my word and I healed your disease

I am the Lord your Healer

You are the God that healeth me

You are the Lord my Healer

*You **sent your word and you healed my***

disease

*You **are the Lord** my **Healer.***

(PRAYER POI NTS)

1. Any power planning to steal. to kill and to destroy me, be consume by fire in Jesus name (Ex 23:25)

2. Every spirit of sickness, in my body, release me in Jesus name

3. Every evil power, running through my body, I loose your grip now, in Jesus name

4. Any power working on my eyes, and lowering my vision, I cast you out completely, in Jesus name.

5. Every spirit of drowsiness, tiredness, and impaired vision, depart from me now, in Jesus name (Psalm 73:26)

6. 1 release myself from every spirit of infirmity, generating tiredness in me. I

bind and cast you out, in Jesus name (Joel 3:10)

7. Every spirit of weight loss and rashes in my body depart from me, in the name of Jesus-Christ.

8. Every spirit of kidney disease, enlargement of the liver, convulsion and loss of consciousness, 1 bind you, in the name of Jesus Christ.

9. Every negative material, running through my body system, I flushed you out, in Jesus name.

10. I bind every spirit of itching, slow healing of cuts, and bruises, in Jesus name.

11. I reject every foreign material, in my blood, in Jesus name.

12. Oh Lord, speak healing and deliverance unto my life in Jesus name

13. Holy Spirit, stretch out your miracle hand and your deliverance hand upon my life

now, in Jesus name. (1 Pet. 2:24, Ps. 37:39-40).

14. I rebuke every grip and refuge of sickness upon my life. in Jesus name (James 5:14)

15. I shall sick no more in Jesus name (Ps. 107:20)

16. Oh Lord, let your whirlwind scatter every vessel of infirmity fashioned against me, in Jesus name

17. Father Lord, let every agent of sickness, working against my health, and every germs of infirmity in my body, die, in Jesus name.

18. Oh Lord, let every fountain of discomfort in my life dry now in Jesus name.

19. Every organ in 'my body, I recover you from every evil altar, in Jesus name. (1 King 13:2)

20. Holy Ghost fire, boil every infirmity out of my system and destroy every stubborn

agents of disease in my body, in Jesus name.

21. Every negative material circulating in blood stream be evacuated in Jesus name.

22. Oh Lord, let earth vomit everything that has been buried inside it, in Jesus name.

23. Father Lord, let the whirlwind of God blow away every wind of infirmity in my body in Jesus name

24. Oh Lord, cancel every clinical prophecy concerning my life, in Jesus name.

25. All the evil plantation in my life, I uproot you, come out sow, in Jesus name (Matt 15:13)

26. Every spirit with tentacles moving about in my body, come out now by fire in Jesus name

27. 1 bind every spirit of bed wetting in Jesus name

28. Oh God my father, let your deliverance hand be stretched out upon my life now in Jesus name.

29. Every knee of infirmity in my life, bow in the name of Jesus

30. Every internal disorder in my life, receive order now in Jesus name

31. Every infirmity, come out with all your roots in the name of Jesus

32. 1 withdraw from every consciousness and unconsciousness cooperation with sickness in Jesus name

33. Oh God, let the whirlwind of God blow every wind of infirmity away, in my life in Jesus name

34. You spirit of itching, I command you to depart from me now, in the mighty name of Jesus

35. I arrest the demon of terminal disease, in my life in Jesus name

FINANCIAL BREAKTHROUGH PRAYER

Bible Reading: Phil 4:19, Jer. 29:11, Heb. 4:16, Job 36:11

(PRAYER POINTS)

1. Catch fire now, every satanic mortar pounding my breakthrough, in Jesus name

2. Every power behind the source of my problems die now, in Jesus name

3. I declare to my business, begin to attract customers now. From the four square of the earth which is the North. South, East and the West, in Jesus name (2 Sam 22:29)

4. All my debtors, begin to look for me now, wherever you might be, to pay me, in Jesus name (2 Kings 8:6)

5. All what I have lost, in my business in the past years, I recover them back now, in Jesus name (1 Pet 5:10)

6. 1 closed the doors of my business to robbers, fraudsters and cheats, in Jesus name

7. 1 receive express attention for my visa application for international business now in Jesus name.

8. Father Lord, let my business frontiers be expand as you did for Jabez in Jesus name

9. I receive express attention, for my application for bank overdraft and loan now in Jesus name

10. Any evil spirit that is causing my money to disappear mysteriously catch fire now, in Jesus name

11. I come against every spirit of loss in my business, in Jesus name

12. I protect my business from any economical meltdown, in Jesus name

13. I cover my business, workshop, office with the blood of Jesus, in Jesus name. (1Pet 1: 19)

14. I claim all my gratuities, pensions and increase in my salary, in Jesus name

15. I declare all the banks in which I have deposits, free from liquidations in Jesus name.

16. Any power sending my money into demonic bank in Jesus name

17. International business partners shall locate me this year in Jesus name

18. I claim credit facilities from my supplier in Jesus name (Ps 30:5)

19. My application for visa on international business received express attention now in Jesus name

20. My shares and bonds i bank, multiply in value in Jesus name

NOTE:- Always pay your tithes and sow

seeds to attract a quick answer to your prayer.

PRAYER FOR SUCCESS IN EXAMINATION

Bible Reading: EccI.**10:10, Isaiah 60:1, Gen 24:12**

PRAYER points

1. Oh Lord, tell me what to read in my preparation for my forthcoming exams, in Jesus name

2. Father, give me the spirit of remembrance so that I will remember all what I read on the exam day (John 14:26)

3. Oh Lord, give me the spirit of remembrance, so that I will remember all what! read on the exam day (John 14:26)

4. Oh Lord, select for me, the right question to write, on the exam day, in Jesus name

5. All the questions that will come out in the exam shall be set from what I read, in Jesus name.

6. I reject the spirit of confusion and distraction in the exam hall, in Jesus name.

7. Oh Lord, let the marker of my scripts, mark with fear of God. in Jesus name (Job 28:28).

8. I reject result seizure for my centre in Jesus name.

9. I cancel the outbreak of fracas in our exam hail, in Jesus name

10. I reject failure and story of missing scripts in my centre, in Jesus name (Job 22:28).

11. Father tell me what to write on examination day.

12. Heavenly father, bless me with good an understanding invigilator and examiner in Jesus name.

13. I claim sound health throughout the period of preparation and written of my examination in Jesus name (Ex 23:25).

PRAYER WHEN LOOKING FOR A LIFE PARTNER

Bible Reading: Gen 2:23, Proverb 18:22

PRAYER POINTS)

1. Oh Lord, I need a woman/man to build a decent home with that will be my life partner (EccI.4:11).

2. I command every power causing a delay in my marital life to be destroyed in Jesus name.

3. Oh Lord, destroy every yoke of hardship that is hindering my efforts to get the man/woman of my desire, by fire, in Jesus name.

4. I open every door of favour closed against my marital life in Jesus name.

5. I break every yoke of difficulty, making my life difficult for me to be engaged in Jesus name. (Isaiah 10:27)

6. Father, I thank you for keeping me alive up to this day, to see the man/woman my heart desire (Man 19:5)

7. Father, I thank you for blessing me with that man/woman who is like a brother/sister, uncle/auntie, father/mother and husband/wife to me (Eph. 5:28)

8. I thank you Lord for the doors of marriage you have opened to me

9. Father Lord, let the man/woman that I am going into marriage with be my husband/wife and not another person's in Jesus name (Ps. 37:4)

10. I declare every enemy of success against my marital plan be frustrated, disgraced and be ashamed now, inn Jesus name (Job 5:12)

11. Every spirit of hindrance causing one problem or the other to arise, to hinder my proposed marriage, receive

earthquake and thunder now! Jesus name (Isaiah 29:6)

12. I washed away every mark of hatred, seeking to hinder my marital blessings, by the Blood of Jesus, in Jesus name.

13. Every spirit of temptation. subjecting my intended husband/wife to actions and behaviours that may kill our proposed marriage, die now in Jesus name (Matt 4:1)

14. I destroy every garment of failure, covering my marital life, in Jesus name

15. Every spirit monitoring and reporting my marriage plans to the satanic kingdoms, die now in Jesus name.

16. Every marine husband/wife that is standing in the way of my marital life, catch fire now in Jesus name

17. I release every power, holding my prospective husband/wife either on the

air, on the land, or in the sea, by fire now in Jesus name.

18. I break every covenant I entered into, knowingly or unknowingly, which is disturbing my marital life, by fire in Jesus name (Amos 3:33).

19. Father Lord, let my dream of a life partner come true soonest in Jesus name (Prov. 18:22).

20. Oh Lord, I command every power causing delay in my marital life to be destroyed in Jesus name.

21. Father cause every evil hand against my marital life to wither in Jesus name.

22. Every evil power working against my marital life plan, bow now.

23. All satanic gang up against my marital life to be destroyed now and forever in Jesus name.

24. Every household enemy sitting on my marital breakthrough die now in Jesus

name (Matt 10:36)

PRAYER FOR MARITAL SUCCESS

Bible Reading: Prov. 26:20,

Corinthians 13:4-5,

I Peter3:8,Eph.5:21-23

(PRAYER POINTS)

1. God the Father, God the son and God the Holy Spirit. I thank you.

2. Oh Lord, I bless and honour your name for my intended marriage.

3. Father, I thank you for bringing my partner and 1 into your divine marital love and understanding (Prov.18:22) .

4. Father, 1 give you glory, honour and adoration for preserving my life and that of my prospective partner (Eph. 5:31).

5. I command every household enemy against my marriage, be destroyed now in Jesus name (Deut. 28:7).

6. Every enemy working hard to tear my marriage apart, die now in Jesus name (Isaiah 54:17).

7. 1 command every evil eye on my family, get blinded now, in Jesus name (Ps. 91:3).

8. 1 scatter every satanic gang up against my marriage now in Jesus name (1 Kings 13:2-3)

9. Every evil temptation on my husband/Wife to go into bad company, disappear flow in Jesus name.

10. I command every charm or concoction prepared by the enemy to tear my family apart, catch fire now, in Jesus name.

11. Every blackmailers against my marriage be disgraced in Jesus name (Isaiah 54:17).

12. Every spirit of miscarriage and barrenness, steer clear of my marriage, in Jesus name (Ps. 128:3).

13. Every weapon formed against my marriage be it unfruitfulness, sickness, quarrel or suspicion, shall be destroyed in Jesus name (Isaiah 54:17).

14. Every spirit of anger and stubbornness, steer clear of my marriage, I bind you in Jesus name (Matt 18:18).

15. I receive divine blessing of male and female children in Jesus name (Deut. 7:14).

16. Every evil storm gathering against my marriages scatter now in Jesus name (Ikings 59:19).

17. You wife or husband snatcher, be disgraced now in Jesus name.

18. All gossiping agent telling my wife or husband one false thing or the other about me be disgraced I Jesus name

PRAYER FOR GOING INTO COURTSHIP

Bible Reading: Matt. 19:6, Gen. 2:23 (PRAYER POINTS)

1. Father, I thank you, for this man/woman you have brought into my life (Prov. 18:22).

2. Oh Lord, you alone know the minds and hearts of men. Please reveal to me the true mind and spirit of this man/woman (mention his/her name).

3. Oh Lord, if this relationship I am going into is not of you. show me a sign (Acts 5 12-14).

4. Father Lord, if the courtship I am going into with (mention his/her name) will not be favourable to me. Please stop it.

5. Father deliver me from every temptations that may put me to shame in this relationship, in Jesus name.

6. Father, Lord. Let this relationship lead us to a successful wedlock, if it truly has

your approval, in Jesus name (Matt 19:4-5).

7. Father, let this courtship put a new song of love and marital understanding into our mouths, in Jesus name (Rev. 5:9).

8. Abraham, Solomon and David blessings shall be our portion at the end of our courtship, in Jesus name (Gal.3:14).

9. I declare that we shall remain under the canopy of the Almighty God throughout the duration of our courtship in Jesus name (Ps. 91:1).

10. I reject every spirit of disappointment and frustration in our relationship, in Jesus name.

11. Father, I refuse to be identify with any relationship that is not ordained by God

12. Any man or woman whom the devil want to use to make my relationship bitter disappear in Jesus name

PRAYER FOR COUPLES ABOUT

TO WED

Bible Reading: Gen. 2:18, Matt. 19:5-6

(PRAYER POINTS)

1. Father, thank you for giving me the love of my life (Gen 2:18)

2. Oh Lord, receive my thanksgiving offering for making my wedding dream a reality (John 2:1-10)

3. Father, Son, Holy Spirit, provide for us, make this our wedding a huge success in Jesus name (Ps 34-10)

4. Oh Lord, I commit my wedding plans to your protective hands, in Jesus name

5. All evil wish against my business/job, my wife's/husband's business/job or against our finances, fail in Jesus name

6. Father, make my marriage financially, physically and spiritually fruitful in Jesus name (Gen. 1:28)

7. I cover my wedding with Blood of Jesus

8. Oh Lord, I bind all the enemy from wife/husband side, disagreeing with my wedding in Jesus name

9. 1 declare, every tongue rising in condemnation of marriage, shrink now, in Jesus name

10. I reject every disappointment/failure of any kind, as my wedding day is fast approaching, in Jesus name

11. I claim mercy and favour from both man and woman to bless me on my wedding day, in Jesus name (Psalm 5:12)

12. I condemn every spirit of jealousy and evil plan against my wedding by fire, in Jesus name

PRAYER FOR TRAVELERS

Bible Reading: Matt. 23:15, Dent. 28:16

(PRAYER POINTS)

1. Oh Lord, I thank you for the journey 1 am about to embark on, 1 know it is your will (Gen 28:20)

2. I called upon the Holy Spirit and the presence of Almighty God, to go with me in this journey, in Jesus name (Matt 1:8,Jer. 1:10)

3. Every road junction inhabiting spirits which wields one evil power or the other on road users, receive the fire of God now, in Jesus name

4. I cover our bus/car and the driver with the blood of Jesus (1 John 1:7)

5. I cover the road with the blood of Jesus, and send every contrary spirit in it packing, in Jesus name

6. Every blood sucking demon on our road, 1 cast you out to be consumed by fire, in Jesus name (Luke 9:1, Matt. 17:18)

7. I command any passenger in our midst, that is an agent of accident, catch fire now, in Jesus name

8. Every evil spirits in the bushes and rivers on our road, remain calm as our vehicle passes you by, in Jesus name.

9. No part of our vehicle, be it the brake, the tyre, the mirrors and the lamps, shall suffer any breakdown/failure in Jesus name

10. Any curse-carrying person, whose presence in our vehicle may affect the smoothness of our journey, shall not travel with us in Jesus name (Matt 25:41)

Blood of Jesus cover our road and send any contrary spirit on parking in Jesus name

PRAYER AGAINST THE SPIRIT OF DEATH/UNTIMELY DEATH

Bible Reading: Ps. 102:1-12, 1 Peter 3:13-18, Isaiah 25:8-9, Ps 13:3-5

Lest my enemy say, "I have prevailed against him". Lest those who troubled me rejoice when I am moved. But I have trusted in your mercy; My heart shall rejoice in your salvation (Ps.13:3-5)

Notes Fast for three days (6:00am — 3:00 pm) to achieve a quick and best result from this prayer

(PRAYER POINT)

1. Every engagement with the spirit of death, I cancel it now, in Jesus name (1Cor. 15:54)

2. I break every evil altar constructed against me into pieces now, in Jesus name (1King 13:2)

3. Oh Lord, let every contractors of death begin to kill themselves, in Jesus name

4. Depart from me now, you spirit of fear of death, in Jesus name (Isaiah 25:8, Psalm 23:4)

5. Oh Lord, cloth me, with the blood of Jesus, and shield me from every bodily harm, in Jesus name (Ps. 86:14-16)

6. Father, deliver me from all household killer, hired to destroy my life, in Jesus name (Gen 9:6)

7. Oh Lord, I trust in you, I shall tread upon the lion and the cobra, and nothing shall harm me by any means, in Jesus name(Ps. 91:13)

8. I reject every spirit of premature death for me and my family, old age is our portions in Jesus name (Zech. 8:4)

9. Any arrow of death, directed to me, I return you back to the sender now, in Jesus name (Ps. 91:4)

10. I bind every blood sucking demon coming to afflict mc. be consumed by fire now, in Jesus name (Matt. 17:18)

11. My husband/Wife shall not die young, my children shall not die young and I

shall not die young, we shall all live to reap the fruits of our labour, and see our children's children, in Jesus name.

12. I command every physical weapon of death, fashioned against me by the enemy, cease to function, in Jesus name (Isaiah 54:17)

13. You witches and wizard that is after my life die now in Jesus name (Ex 22:18)

14. Every evil alter constructed against me, break into pieces now in Jesus name (1 king 13:2)

You road accident, water accident, aircraft that may wanted claim my life when it is not yet time for me to die I cancel you by holy ghost fire in Jesus name

PRAYER FOR DELIVERANCE FROM FOUNDATIONAL BOUNDAGE

Bible Reading: Ga15:1, Matt. 8:17, Ex.

13:14

(PRAYER POINTS)

1. Oh Lord, let your power of deliverance, fall upon me now, in Jesus name

2. I break every yoke of foundational curse in life now, in Jesus name (Gal. 3:13)

3. Every foundational influences in my life, I break you by the blood of Jesus now, in Jesus name

4. Every foundational familiar spirit and marine power, I bind and cast you out now, in Jesus name

5. Every scorpion and serpent in my life foundation, die now, in Jesus name (Gen. 3:1-6)

6. I break every foundational covenant in my life, in Jesus name

7. Holy spirit, break down every fundamental stronghold and confusion in my life, in Jesus name

8. Oh God, arise and let every seed of witchcraft and foundation of witchcraft scatter and die, in Jesus name (Exo. 22:18)

9. Every foundation of darkness planted in my life, turn to light now, in Jesus name (John1 5)

10. Every seed of poverty and foundational padlock in my life, break now and die, in Jesus name (2 Cor. 8:9, Isaiah 10:27)

11. Every evil cry of any idol fashioned against me, I silence you now, in Jesus name

12. I lose every hold of idol in my father's house, in my life, in Jesus name

13. Any strong man of the idol in my father's house, die now in Jesus name

14. Every family idols from both sides of my parents, release me now, in Jesus name (Exo20:3)

15. Father, heal every disease of our family altars in Jesus name

16. I remove myself from every curses and territorial spirit, in Jesus name (Isaiah 10:27)

17. I refuse to follow every evil pattern programmed by any of my ancestors, in Jesus name

18. Oh Lord, turn back to the foundation of my life and carry out every necessary surgical operation

19. Any satanic trademark on my family, be erased now, in Jesus name

20. Oh Lord, let your sword of deliverance, cut down the tree of every family afflictions in my life, in Jesus name (Eph. 6:17, Hosea 2:18)

21. Every foundational arrester, be arrested in the name of Jesus

22. Every foundational bondage in my life break now, in Jesus name

23. Every seed of witchcraft in my foundational, die now in the name of Jesus

24. Oh God my father, let every foundation of confusion in my life crash now in Jesus name

25. Every foundational marine power bow now in Jesus name

26. Every seed of poverty in my foundation, die in Jesus name.

PRAYER TO CANCEL BAD DREAMS

Bible Reading: Joel 2:28, Matt. 27:19, Matt. 2:13, JoW33:lS

(PRAYER POINTS)

1. Father, I know that dream is one of the way in which you talk to your children. Help me to have dreams and not bad Ones tonight, in Jesus name (Joel 2:28, Acts 2:17)

2. Every night afflictions and oppressions in my life, cease now, in Jesus name

3. Every spirit of bad dreams, die now and cease to afflict me, in Jesus name

4. Every spiritual covenant that 1 have enter into on my behalf, by my parents, which exposes me to the danger of bad dreams, be broken now, in Jesus name (Amos 3:3)

5. Every avenues of eating or drinking poisons spiritually, be closed now, in Jesus name

6. I break every spiritual covenant I entered into, knowingly or unknowingly which exposes me to dreadful dreams, in Jesus name (Amos 3:3)

7. I cancel every bad dreams that is not of God in Jesus name

8. You agents and spirit of bad dreams, pack your load and go now, in Jesus name

9. I refuse the experience of eating, drinking, marrying, sexing, quarrelling

fighting in the dream, shall never be my
portion as from today, in Jesus name

10. Every spirit of sicknesses that arise to bad
dreams. disappear now, in Jesus name
(Prov. 18:14, Matt 8:17)

11. I Cover myself with the blood of Jesus,
and to shield me away from bad dreams

12. I reject every family and village
fetishes/shrines that I encounter in my
dreams catch fire now, in Jesus name.

13. You spirit of sickness, making me prone
to bad dreams, disappear now in Jesus
name (Jer. 30:17)

14. You spiritual wife or husband that keeps
disturbing me in my dream in Jesus name

15. All family and village fetishes or shrines
that I encounter in dream catch fire now
in Jesus name (Exo.20:3)

16. I refuse to have any sleep in which I will
be afflicted with bad dream

Bible Reading: Ps. 23:5, 1 Cor. 15:25, Isaiah 41:10, Malt 10:36, Heb. 10:13, Deut. 31:6 "Be strong and of good courage, do not fear, nor be afraid of the,,,, for the lord 'our God, He is the one who goes wit!, you. He will not leave you nor forsake you "Deut. 31:6)
You prepare a table before me in the presence of my enemies; you anoint my head with, oil, my cup runs over (Ps. 23:5)

(PRAYER POINTS)

1. Oh Lord, let every rage of my enemies be quenched, in Jesus name (Isaiah 59:19)
2. Every oracle boasting against me, I silence you now, in Jesus name (Ps. 91:3)
3. Every enemies of progress, remain beggars all the days of your lives, in Jesus name

4. Father, I know that you are my maker,
   please do not forsake me, for my enemies
   have closed in on me (Ps 138:8)

5. I refuse to become what my enemies want
   me to become, in Jesus name (Ps. 89:22)

6. I silence every power crying, saying "It's
   over" upon my life, in Jesus name

7. Anybody, who envy my wealth, and who
   spend sleepless nights thinking about
   how to take what belongs to me. Die
   now, in Jesus name

8. All evil thought fashioned against me by
   the enemy, be disgraced now, in Jesus
   name (Isaiah 54:17)

9. All evil candle burning against me, die
   now, in Jesus name

10. I empty every boasting of the enemies
    against me now, in Jesus name (Luke 9:1)

11. Arise, lion of Judah, according to your
    name and pursue all my pursuers, in Jesus
    name (Rev 5:5)

12. Oh Lord, let the poison of the serpents and scorpions fashioned against me, die now in Jesus name.

13. Every bad tongue, speaking evil against my life, be pulled outflow, in Jesus name (Isa 54:17)

14. Every enemy who wish me evil, that are supposed to die for my star to shine, die now, in Jesus name.

15. Oh God my father let all my enemies who envy my wealth and who spend sleepless nights thinking about how to take what to belong to me be condemn to poverty in Jesus name

PRAYER AGAINST DELAY IN MARRIAGE

PRAYER POINTS

1. Every satanic mirror monitoring my marital destiny, catch the lire of the Holy Ghost now in Jesus name.

2. Every demonic hand pulling down my joyful day of marriage is cut off now by the sword of the Spirit in the name of Jesus Christ.

3. 0 God let your mercies prevail over my marital destiny in Jesus name.

4. Arise 0 God and let every barrier standing on my way to the altar be scattered in Jesus name.

5. Father, let every hidden covenant manipulating my glorious day of marriage be destroyed by the blood of Jesus Christ.

6. O You spirit of delay in marriage, I command the fire of the Holy Ghost upon you right and be burnt into ashes in the name of Jesus Christ.

7. Because God said loneliness is not good, therefore every effort of hell trying to keep me single, catch fire now in Jesus name.

8. It is written, none shall lack her mate, so therefore I come against every power that is keeping my marital partner in Jesus name.

9. It is written, light shines in darkness and the darkness comprehend it not. Whatever that is keeping me in the darkness of life. Preventing my partner from seeing me, catch fire right now in the name of Jesus.

10. Precious Father, I thank you because you have heard me. I praise you *for* taking the glory on my wedding day in Jesus name I have prayed (Amen).

PRAYERS AGAINST TENSION IN MARRIAGE
PRAYER POINTS

1. Read 2Chronicles 20:30 and begin to command supernatural rest for your marriage.

2. Read Numbers 6:26 and say, 0 peace of the Most High, I command you to rest upon my marriage in the name of Jesus Christ.

3. Read Joshua 9:15, then ask the Holy Spirit to bring peace between you and your partner in Jesus Christ name.

4. Read Leviticus 6:5 and challenge Satan of being guilty, then authoritatively ask him to return the peace, rest, love and harmony he has stolen from your marriage in Jesus Christ name.

5. Every-manipulation from the pit of hell working against my marriage, catch fire of the Holy Ghost in the name of Jesus Christ.

6. Read Psalm 5 1:12 and tell the Lord to restore unto you the joy of your marriage as it was in the beginning.

7. Read Song of Solomon 1:2 and say, O lord, Let my partner's love and romance

be kindled for me again in the name of Jesus Christ.

8. O Lord deal with me in any area I need to be dealt with and give me grace to tolerate my partner in Jesus name.

9. You wicked spirit of separation and divorce; I curse you over my marriage in the name of Jesus Christ.

10. Give thanks to God for answering your prayers and make effort to stir up romance between you and partner.

PRAYER FOR SUCCESSFUL DELIVERY OF A CHILD

Confession: Psalm 18, Numbers 23:23, Isa. 66:7-8

1. Every satanic mirror monitoring my day of delivery catch fire and scatter in Jesus name

2. Every satanic or demonic spirit that wants make mc weak in the labour room roast by fire in Jesus name.

3. All efforts from the pit of hell that want to disposition my body, die by fire in Jesus name.

4. Father, I decree that my labour shall not be complicated and difficult in Jesus name

5. Arise for me 0 God and let every satanic barrier against me and my unborn child scatter in Jesus name

6. I receive strength from above to push and bring forth in Jesus name

7. I receive strength from above to be fearless in Jesus name

8. I become touch not for any nurse or doctor, who is an agent of devil in Jesus name

9. Lord, I receive power to leap over all the walls of complication on my delivery day in Jesus name.

10. Holy spirit, as you enable Mary to bring forth Jesus. enable mc to bring forth my child in Jesus name

11. I cover every hospital equipment that will be used on mc with the blood of Jesus.

12. As you covered Elisha with chariot of fire; Father,] cover the labour room that I will use with he fire of the Holy Ghost. No arrow of the enemy shall be able to pass through in Jesus name

13. O Lord, lets all that will be needed: spiritually, physically, medically or Biological be supplied by the hosts of heaven in Jesus name

14. Father. I come against any form of death before, during and after my lab our in Jesus name.

15. I shall laugh at those who plotting evil against me in Jesus name

16. I decree and declare, my labour shall be like of the Hebrew women in Jesus might name.

17. As leafs fall off tree, and the tree does not complain of pain, so shall my delivery be in Jesus name.

18. Lord, send your angels into the labour room ahead of me and let them minister into me in Jesus name.

19. Anything under the sun that want to destabilize my health on or before my labour, be roasted by fire of the Holy Ghost

20. Lord Jesus, let your favour surprise and surpass all medical theories concerning me.

PRAYER FOR THE FRUIT OFTHE WOMB

Psalm 127:4-5. As arrows are in the hand of a mighty man, so are children of the youth.

Happy is the man that hath his quiver full of them: they shall not be ashamed, but they shall speak with the enemies in the gate!

PRAYER POINT

1. Every plantation of darkness fired into my womb in the dream, your time is up expire melt away by fire in the name of Jesus (Psalm 127:3)

2. Arrows of fruitfulness locate and uproot every gate of barrenness in my life, in Jesus name.

3. Arrows of fruitfulness, arise and kill every shame of barrenness in my Life in the labour of my hands in Jesus name

4. Enemies of my fruitfulness, what are you waiting for? Die now in Jesus name.

5. Voice of barrenness, speaking against my fruitfulness shut up now and die in the mighty name of Jesus.

6. As a believers that knows the prayer works, lay your hand on your womb as

you take this prayer: my womb, hear the word of the Lord, conceive, Nurture and bear my children according to the time of life in Jesus name (Ps 128:3)

7. This year, I lay hold on the key to a fruitful and prosperous family life in Jesus name.

8. This year, I inherit from the lord of Host, a flourishing family in the name of Jesus.

9. Every wicked arrow of ungodliness, impurity and iniquity fired against my fruitfulness, perish by fire in the name of Jesus (Gen 18:14)

10. Is anything too hard for the lord? No! of Heaven will return to me, about this time next year, i (mentioned your name) shall be dancing and playing with my son or daughter in the mighty name of Jesus

PRAYER AGAINST SPIRITUAL ATTACK

This is not a physical battle, rather it is a spiritual one that requires spiritual understanding, the understanding here is that the fact that you don't see this battle or its effect in your life does not mean that it is not there. Therefore, pray these prayers defensively as if in a real battle. The lord of victory will certainly give you victory in Jesus name.

NOTE: Pray those prayers mostly in the middle of the night and pay with Psalm *35*.

PRAYER POINT

1. Every spiritual activity of darkness against my life, be fruitfulness in Jesus name.

2. I paralyze every effort of wickedness targeted against my destiny in the name of Jesus.

3. Every principalities and powers on assignment concerning my life and my destiny be arrested in Jesus name.

4. Oh Lord, deliver me from every witchcraft manipulation designed to pull me down in life in the name of Jesus.

5. Every weapon of satanic attack engaged against my life, be wasted in Jesus name.

6. I raise a standard against every attack of rulers of darkness in my life in Jesus name.

7. Oh Lord my father, shield my family with the blood of Jesus from every from of spiritual attacks in Jesus name.

8. Heavenly father, attack every spiritual attackers attacking my destines in the name of Jesus.

9. 1 reject every spiritual manipulation and operations in my dream from today in the name of Jesus.

10. Father, by the Holy Ghost fire, make my life un-attackable in Jesus name.